THE LONELY  LITTLE TREE

A story for all ages

SHEELAGH MAWE

TOTALLY UNIQUE THOUGHTS

P. O. Box 2962, Windermere, FL 34786-2962

More from Totally Unique Thoughts®
at www.tut.com or at bookstores everywhere:

Dandelion
The Extraordinary Life of a Misfit
Hardcover and Paperback, Sheelagh Mawe,
1994, 2004

How Mom Got a Life
Paperback, Sheelagh Mawe, 2005

Totally Unique Thoughts
Reminders of Life's Everyday Magic
Paperback, Mike Dooley, 1998

Lost in Space
Paperback, Mike Dooley, 1998

Thoughts Become Things * LIVE!
Audio Tape/CD, Mike Dooley, 2001

Infinite Possibilities
The Art of Living Your Dreams
Audio Program, Mike Dooley, 2002

Notes from the Universe
Hardback Books 1-3, Mike Dooley, 2003

THE LONELY LITTLE TREE

Published by Totally Unique Thoughts®
a Division of TUT® Enterprises, Inc.
Orlando, Florida • www.tut.com

Book Design and Illustrations by Kathy Harestad,
www.KathyArt.com

Library of Congress Control Number: 2006929274

ISBN   0-9765420-6-4

Printed in Canada

If every tree

tried to look like another,

they'd forget that they're special

and unlike any other.

– Mike Dooley –

For all who marvel at nature.

THE LONELY LITTLE TREE

All alone …

THE LONELY LITTLE TREE

… in a vast meadow, grew a tree. It was a very young, very small tree, scarcely taller than the grasses that grew around it.

And because it was alone, the only tree as far as the eye could see, it did not know the way of trees, nor even that it was a tree. All it knew was that it was.

That, and the great, ever-changing sky above it with its shining sun and gleaming moon, its million stars and tumbling clouds. And all day, every day, it yearned towards that sky, thinking it a most beautiful and wondrous thing.

So intrigued, in fact, was the tree with the glory above it that for a very long time it was unaware of its own growth upwards or the silent spread of its roots growing strong and deep in the earth below.

But one day, bowing low beneath the worst storm in the memory of the meadow, the tree was astonished to discover that where before it had only one slender trunk, now, miraculously, branches grew in all directions from that thickened, sturdy trunk, and each branch was laden with the most beautiful leaves.

THE LONELY LITTLE TREE

Well ... right away the tree forgot all about the sky and the sun and the moon and the stars and turned all its attention to the magnificence of itself.

And as it observed, it came to understand a most amazing and wonderful thing, which was that while each leaf was a part of the tree, it was "itself," too, unique, and unlike any of the other leaves, though all grew from the same source.

Another thing it came to understand was that each leaf had an entirely different view — and therefore, knowledge — of the meadow. One growing on an upper branch facing north, for example, would have little understanding of the small creatures and insects that scampered about in the undergrowth of ferns and flowers below.

While a leaf on a lower limb, facing south, would know next to nothing about the many flocks of birds, and even bats, that sped by, or of changes in temperature and the direction of wind currents.

But because of them, the tree at their center knew all their viewpoints and each was as important and cherished by it as the next. And the tree loved all its leaves dearly, the way a parent loves its children, however different and varied their attitudes and outlooks might be.

All through the soft days of spring and the hot days of summer, the tree gloried in its leaves and learned from them and basked in their loveliness.

But gradually, without the tree ever noticing, the days grew shorter and the sun lost its warmth. The tree didn't notice because it had more important things to think about just then, and that was that all of its leaves, which it had always known as green, were mysteriously turning into the most glorious shades of yellow and gold and scarlet and crimson, and the tree was bewitched by their beauty.

How wonderful, it thought, that of everything growing in this meadow, I am at the center of all this magnificence. And it was so happy it didn't notice that the wind, which it had always known as a gentle friend, was growing stronger and colder, until one day a terrible thing happened: one of its leaves, fluttering and dancing at the end of a limb, suddenly let go and, without a backward glance, floated away with the wind.

"Stop!" the tree cried out in dismay. "You can't fly away like that! Your place is here! You are a part of me! Why, without you I am less than I was. Come back!"

But even as the tree cried out, other leaves let go, too, and followed after the first, and there was nothing the tree could do, nothing it could say, to make them stop.

Day after miserable day, as the wind grew colder and howled through its branches, the leaves continued to fly away, some in ones and twos, as though reluctant to part, others in great flurries, seeming eager to follow in the path of the wind.

Until there came a day, a terrible day, when the tree was without any leaves at all and it stood alone and shivering in the bitter cold.

THE LONELY LITTLE TREE

"A fine friend you turned out to be," it called out in anguish to the wind. "Look what you've done to me! You've taken away everything I loved and tossed them far and wide and now what's to become of me? Without my leaves to love and admire and learn from, I am nothing and I have nothing to do."

But the wind only laughed as it sped by. "Have patience, little tree," it called, "and rest while you can, for by-and-by, in the spring, I shall return softly and you will be surprised at how much everything will have changed."

But the tree, who was very young and had little memory of past winters or springs, didn't understand and cried out instead to the sky, the only other thing it had ever known.

"I don't understand why this happened to me," it sobbed. "I really loved my leaves and I can't bear to be without them ... It's too lonely ... Can you tell me what to do or why I must stay here all alone?"

But the sky was dark and gray and tumbled by the wind itself and had no answer for the tree.

Then the tree had a wonderful idea and turned back eagerly to the wind. "I know just what to do!" it called. "Take me with you and let me see where it is you go for surely it must be a wonderful place that everything hurries to join you on your journey."

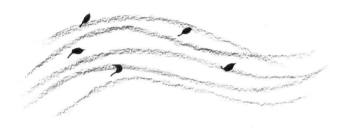

"Some must go and some must stay," the wind roared. "You must stay, for that is the way of trees. And I must go because the way of the wind is to be forever in motion.

"On my travels I carry the rains and snows and seeds and scatter them wherever they are needed, even to the far ends of the earth. Indeed, it was I who brought you here to this treeless meadow in the first place and it is I who has carried many of your seeds to other parts of this meadow and even further afield than that!"

"Very impressive, I'm sure," sighed the tree. "But really, it all seems rather pointless to me if in the end I'm to be left all alone and ignorant, forever rooted in this boring place. What is my reason for being here? What is my purpose?"

"This meadow is where you are supposed to be. This is your place and this is your time. And your purpose is the same as all the other species that live and grow upon the face of the earth: to be exactly what they are, which, in your case, is a tree!" howled the wind. "That is all. To be yourself! To be happy! To be proud!"

.

"Of what?" the tree glowered. "For what?" But the wind had no more time to spare and with a flourish disappeared behind a mountain top. And because now there was no sound, no movement in the frozen meadow, nothing to observe, nothing to listen to, the tree, in spite of itself, fell into the long sleep of winter.

The warmth and light of the sun awakened it. Not the pale, cold light of the winter sun, but the soft, warming glow of the spring sun.

The tree stirred and gazed about it and saw that the meadow, which it remembered as barren and frozen, was greening and that new life abounded everywhere.

"Thank you, little tree, for sheltering us this winter," said a mother rabbit, bringing her babies out of a burrow at the tree's base for their first warming rays the sun. "Without your protection we certainly would have perished."

"Why ... it was nothing," said the tree with a smile. "I was here anyway."

"Thank you for your delicious acorns that saved us from hunger all winter," said a sleepy little squirrel, yawning and stretching in the soft air.

THE LONELY LITTLE TREE

"Well goodness gracious!" said the tree. "You mean those funny little things can be eaten?"

"Indeed, they can," said the squirrel. "Why, without them we could not live in this beautiful meadow at all. Surely you remember how busy we were at the end of summer gathering them up quickly before the cold wind could come to scatter them far and wide."

THE LONELY LITTLE TREE

"Yes," the tree nodded, "I do remember. And that was very clever of you for it seems the wind sweeps everything before it. I'm glad you enjoyed them."

"Thank you for your strong branches," chirped a busy little robin. "In this nest I am building high above the ground, my young will be very safe."

"Oh … please make yourself at home," said the tree. "It's nice to know they can serve such a useful purpose."

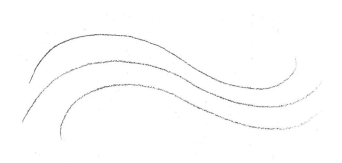

Just then a gentle breeze came to hover above the tree. "Now do you understand why you have to stay?" it whispered. "Do you see how necessary you are to the life of this meadow?

"And do you have any idea how much I will look forward to coming to rest in your cool green shade after a long journey across the rock-strewn mountains? Or the pleasure I take in playing, however briefly, among your beautiful leaves before I continue my journey?"

"Oh, but you're mistaken," the tree said with a sigh. "Surely you remember that you came last autumn and took away all my leaves, scattering them here, there and everywhere. I'm afraid there are none left for you to play among."

The wind chucked. "My young friend," it said. "You have much to learn. Just look at yourself now! Why, you're a vision all decked out in your beautiful new leaves!"

"New leaves?" the tree gasped, drawing itself up tall. And sure enough, all of its branches were filled to bursting with bright, shiny new leaves.

"But ..." the tree stammered. "I ... I don't understand ... Where did they come from?"

"They came from within you," the wind chuckled. "As does all new growth. And every spring for hundreds of years you will send out fresh, new leaves and every autumn I will come to take them away with me, for it is in this way that the old always makes way for the new.

THE LONELY LITTLE TREE

"And as you have now learned, when the winters come, as they always will, you will rest and gather your strength for your next crop of leaves and acorns. And meantime you will provide shelter for the small creatures that live here with you in this meadow."

"But … I still don't understand. What is the reason for all this?" the tree asked.

"It is for you to learn."

"To learn? To learn what?"

"The very special role you have to play in the grand life of the universe. To accept that change is necessary.

"To love and let go. To give of yourself. To understand that you are important, needed and loved. And this, my friend, is true whether you are covered in leaves or not."

"All that?" the tree exclaimed. "That is a lot to learn!"

"Yes, it is," the wind agreed. "But don't worry, every year it will get easier. And as you grow, so will your wisdom until there will come a day when you become a fine example to others."

"Oh … I don't know about that," the tree faltered. "I don't think I'll ever be wise enough or special enough to set an example to others. I mean, come on … I'm only a tree."

"Only a tree, indeed!" the wind exploded. "Why, just as you once noticed that none of your leaves grew exactly like another, so I, endless traveler that I am, can tell you that while there are millions of trees growing upon the earth, some on mountains, some in deserts, some looking down on busy city streets, others on tropical beaches, nowhere, but nowhere, in the world is there another tree just exactly like you."

"Nowhere!" exclaimed the tree. "Good heavens! That does make me feel rather special. In fact, it makes me feel quite unique. Perhaps then ... I mean ... just possibly, I could get used to the idea of setting an example, after all. But what, indeed, who in the world could learn anything from me?"

"Sometimes you try my patience, little tree," the wind snapped. "Surely you must have noticed by now that everything learns from everything else! Think of what you learned from the sky, the clouds, the moon, the stars! And what about the animals? Think of what you learned from them!

"Now, think about all the tiny acorns I scattered last autumn that even now are pushing their way to the surface of this very meadow as you once did. To whom will they will turn, if not you, to learn of themselves?

"Looking ahead even further, you must realize that through them your own knowledge will grow as you see yourself mirrored in them."

"This sounds like it could be fun!" chuckled the little tree.

"It is! It is!" said the wind. "Why, life is the grandest adventure of all! And when you truly understand that every living thing, no matter the differences in appearance, customs, place of birth, way of life, is exactly where it's supposed to be, doing exactly what it's supposed to be doing, then you will have learned the most valuable lesson of all, little tree."

"I will?" gasped the tree. "Quickly. Tell me what it is."

"You will have learned to love and accept yourself exactly the way you are!" said the wind.

"And in doing so, your love will grow to include all other living things, and free you to accept them just exactly as they are

"And that, little tree, is the greatest lesson of all and the reason you are here — to love!"

And with a sw-o-o-osh the wind went laughing away across the mountain top.

THE END

TOTALLY UNIQUE THOUGHTS®

... because thoughts become things!®

Launched in 1989 by two brothers and their cool mom,
TUT® believes that everyone is special, that every life is
meaningful, and that we're all here to learn that dreams
really do come true.

We also believe that "thoughts become things®," and
that imagination is the gift that can bring love, health,
abundance and happiness into our lives.

Totally Unique Thoughts®
TUT® Enterprises, Inc.
Orlando, Florida
www.tut.com
USA